TO

DAVID

LOVE FROM

David dreamed of becoming an astronaut.

He loved rockets.
He knew more about the Moon than his teachers.
And he had collected loads of space toys.

But today David had to think about making space rather than outer space. His bedroom was so messy it looked like an asteroid had hit it.

David carefully sorted through everything and began to fill his rucksack with old toys to take to the shed.

David shuffled out of the house and down the garden path.

And there, resting on a pile of broken planks that used to be the shed, was a shiny metal rocket.

"Woah!" yelled David.

"A SPACE ROCKET! IN MY GARDEN!"

David charged up the ramp and clambered up a ladder to the control room. There was a chair in the centre, and he sat down and spun round and round.

As the chair turned he couldn't believe what he was seeing....

Flashing lights, blinking buttons and long levers surrounded him, and a small alien was hunched over, pulling at the controls.

"Err ... hello?" said David.

The alien turned round and yelped in surprise. He jumped backwards and sat down on the shiniest, reddest button David had ever seen.

The doors slid shut with a *WHOOSH* and a *CLUNK*, and David felt a rumbling that got bigger and bigger and louder and louder.

5 ... 4 ... 3 ... 2 ... 1 ...

"Hold on tight!" the alien yelled. "We're off ..."

LAUNCH
WHEERRPP!!

"... TO THE MOON!"

As they flew through space they quickly became best friends.

The alien told David amazing stories about his travels through the galaxy, and how today he was heading to the dark side of the Moon. He was sure no one had ever explored it before.

The rocket touched down, and after finding a space suit for David to wear they opened the door.

At the last moment David ducked back inside, quickly tipped his rucksack out and pulled it on. Just in case.

"You never know, it may come in handy," he said.

David and the alien bounced around, kicking up puffs of Moon dust and gazing out at the twinkling stars.

"Hang on," said David, as he took a giant leap, "I think I can see ... tyre tracks?!"

"Maybe we're not the first to explore the dark side of the Moon after all," whispered the alien.

"Only one way to find out," replied David.

"LET'S GO!"

They followed the tyre tracks around small craters and huge boulders until they came to the edge of a deep cave.

"What's that at the bottom?" wondered David. The alien slowly lowered him down on the end of a rope, his footsteps echoing around the walls.

CLUMP CLUMP CLUMP CLUMP CLUMP CLUMP

"It looks like a metal glove." He stuffed it in his rucksack and quickly climbed back out.

"This will look great in my space-junk collection!" David cheered.

Soon they came to a spooky Moon cave. The alien looked nervous as he peered into the gloom.

"Don't worry," said David as he rummaged in his rucksack, "I've got my old wind-up rocket torch."

They crept into the vast cave and saw crystals covering every wall from top to bottom. As David was gazing up at the sparkling rocks, he stubbed his toe on something and yelped loudly:

"OUCHYA!"

He knelt down to get a closer look: "Hmm, it's a small wheel."

David stuffed it into his rucksack and they trudged up a narrow slope that led back to the surface.

They soon found themselves on the edge of a canyon. David stared hard – he could see a mini satellite dish glinting on the other side.

"Well, we can't go around it," said the alien. "And I don't think we can jump that far, even with a run-up."

"I've got it!" yelled David, as he gripped the valve on his air tank. "Grab my hand and hold tight."

WHOOOOOSH!

David let out a sudden blast of air and they flew across the canyon, floating gently down on the other side.

"Awesome," he smiled. "I'm going to have the best space-treasure collection ever!"

David was zipping up his rucksack when the alien tapped him on the shoulder.

He looked up and saw the tyre track leading to a huge boulder that had a ginormous shadow stretching out from behind it. The alien gasped:

"YIKES! RUN!"

"Don't worry," said David. "Just stay very, very still...."

As they froze, a cute robot slowly wobbled out from behind the rock, blinking in surprise.

"Hello," smiled David, "are you okay?"

"Hurrr-errr, not really," yawned the space robot. "I've been sleepwalking again and lost a few bits and pieces on the way."

He held out an arm which was missing a hand. He pointed to his leg which was missing a wheel, and then pointed to the side of his head which was missing a mini satellite dish. David gasped.

"HANG ON!"

They carefully took the missing parts out of David's rucksack one by one, while the space robot happily whirred and beeped.

David and the alien helped repair their new friend, and soon the space robot looked his shiny best again.

Out of the corner of his eye David could see Earth, and realised just how much he missed being there: "I think it's time to go home."

They said goodbye to the space robot and began their journey back to the rocket, following their own footsteps.

Over the canyon they went, back through the spooky Moon cave, and around the edge of the deep cave. Soon they were safely back in the control room of the rocket, ready to ...

BLAST OFF!

They slowly rumbled out of the sky into David's garden. The door opened and he walked down the ramp and turned to wave goodbye to his new best friend one last time.

"Come back soon," yelled David.

"I promise," said the alien.

Back in his bedroom, David unzipped his rucksack and stared in surprise at the sparkling Moon rock the alien had left for him.

He gazed back up at the starry sky, hoping that his next BIG adventure would be out of this world.

GO DIVING?
Maybe I'll ...

David, look out for more **Mini Adventures** books.
Go to www.orangutanbooks.com

Story by J.D. Green
Illustrated by Jo Lindley
Designed by Ryan Dunn

orangutan

First published by Orangutan Books in 2019
1 Queen Street, Bath BA1 1HE

www.orangutanbooks.com
Follow us @orangutanbooks

ISBN 978-1-83883-433-3

Printed in Italy
OB_PO201990

FSC
www.fsc.org
MIX
Paper from responsible sources
FSC® C023419